REAL WORLD MATH FOR THINKING KIDS

Measurement Scouts

Using Measurement Tools to Solve Problems

Published in cooperation with
Rolling Readers
San Marco, California

Copyright © 1995 by Scholastic Inc.   All rights reserved. Published by Scholastic Inc.   Printed in U.S.A.
ISBN 0-590-27888-6
2 3 4 5 6 7 8 9 10   09   01 00 99 98 97 96 95

Measurements help us make comparisons and find solutions to problems.

Measurement Scouts

We choose units of measure to compare and communicate size.

Video

SUBCONCEPT

⭐ **1**

We measure things by comparing them to other things.

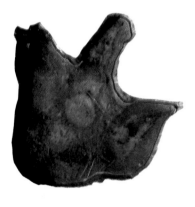

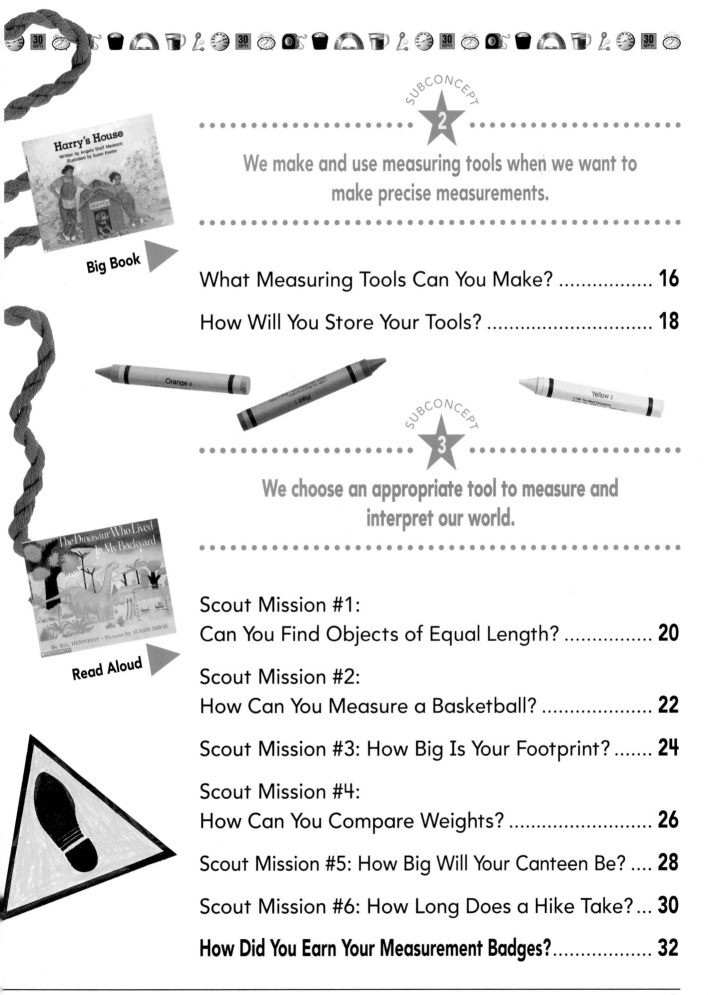

We make and use measuring tools when we want to make precise measurements.

Big Book

We choose an appropriate tool to measure and interpret our world.

Read Aloud

How Big Is Big?

An elephant is pretty big. A gorilla is big, too. A dog is bigger than a cat. A cat is bigger than a mouse. What is a mouse bigger than? How can you tell if something is big?

Explore "bigness."

 DO·iT
- Work with a partner. Put some objects into a paper bag.
- Take two objects out of the bag. Which one is bigger?

SHARE·iT
- Tell the class what you did. How did you decide which object was bigger?

BUILD·ON·iT
- Measure some objects with snap cubes. How many cubes long are they? How many cubes wide are they?

You can use:
Paper bag
Crayons or markers
Snap cubes
Paper
Other objects

THINK
Are you big or small?

5

How Can You Use Your Hands to Measure?

How are these kids measuring this chair?

How many hands wide is the chair?

How many fingers wide is it?

Use your hands.

You can use:
Your hands
Paper
Pencil

 • Work with a partner. Pick something in the classroom. How many hands long or wide is it? Estimate, then find out.

• Tell what you did.

• How close was your estimate?

• Trace your hand with your fingers spread out. Then trace it with your fingers together.

• Use the tracings to measure things.

• How are the measurements different? How are they alike?

table

chair

6 hands and 3 fingers

THINK
Are measurements with your fingers or with your hands more precise? Explain.

How Do You Measure Up?

What is a scout? Scouts explore things. They report what they find. Good scouts keep their eyes open and always look for new things. You can be a measurement scout!

Measure something.

You can use:
✝ Yourself

DO·IT
- Pick objects in your classroom. Estimate how many hands, arms, or feet long they are. Measure the objects.
- Draw pictures of what you measured. Show the measurements you made.

SHARE·IT
- Show your measurements to a partner. Tell how you made them.

BUILD·ON·IT
- Work with a team. Each of you take turns measuring the same thing.
- Compare your measurements.

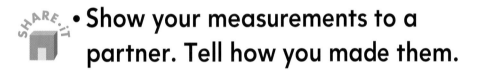

THINK
What words do we use to describe the sizes of things?

9

How Can You Show You Are a Measurement Scout?

What do scouts wear? You can wear a headband to show you are a measurement scout. What size will your headband be?

Measure yourself.

You can use:
- Yarn
- Snap cubes
- Butcher paper
- Construction paper
- Crayons or markers
- Scissors

DO·iT
- How can you measure your head?
- Cut a piece of yarn that is as long as your head is round.

SHARE·iT
- Measure the yarn using cubes or some other unit.
- Make a class display to show the yarn and how long each piece is.

 • Make a headband to show the world you are a measurement scout.
• How do you know what size to make the headband?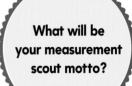

THINK

What will be your measurement scout motto?

How Can Measurements Help You Find Things?

Scouts must be able to find things.
A scout can tell exactly where something
is with directions.

Give directions.

 • Pick an object in your classroom. Plan the route you would take to get from your desk to the object. Measure how many steps away the object is, and how many turns you would make.

• Write directions to the object. Don't say what the object is.

 • Share your directions with a partner. See if you can follow each other's directions.

Start at my desk. Go forward 5 steps. Turn right.

Walk 3 steps towards the window. Turn right.

Walk 2 steps towards the door

Are you at the fish tank?

THINK
How long is the longest straight line you can walk in your classroom?

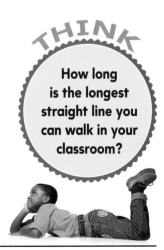

What Is a Measurement Scavenger Hunt?

Get ready to search, scouts. It's time for a measurement scavenger hunt. These are the sorts of clues you will need for the scavenger hunt.

Look for things:

- Smaller than a 👆
- longer than a ✏️ but shorter than an 💪
- bigger than a 😊

Have a hunt.

DO·it
- Work with a partner. Think of measurement clues to describe objects in your class.
- Record your clues. Use words or pictures.

SHARE·it
- Trade clues with another pair of students.
- Start hunting! Find things that meet the clues.
- Can you find more than one thing for each clue? Try it.

BUILD·ON·it
- Compare things that fit the same clue. How are they different? How are they the same?

You can use:
Paper
Pencil

Clifford's FAMILY

SCHOLASTIC
NORMAN BRIDWELL

Yellow 2

Orange 4

THINK
How did you use measurement on your scavenger hunt?

What Measuring Tools Can You Make?

You can use tools to measure more accurately. What could you measure with each of these things?

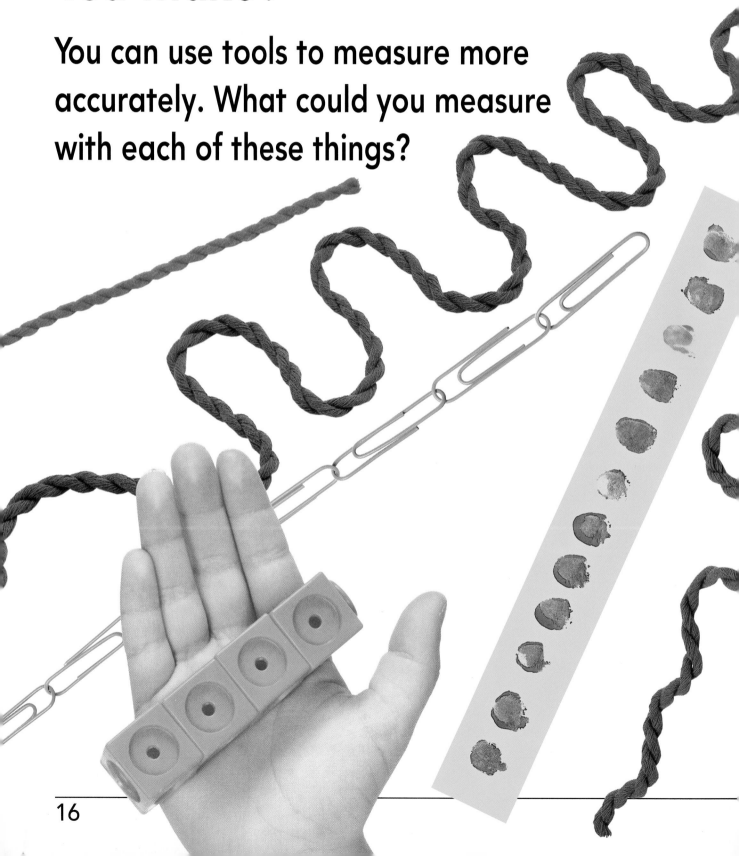

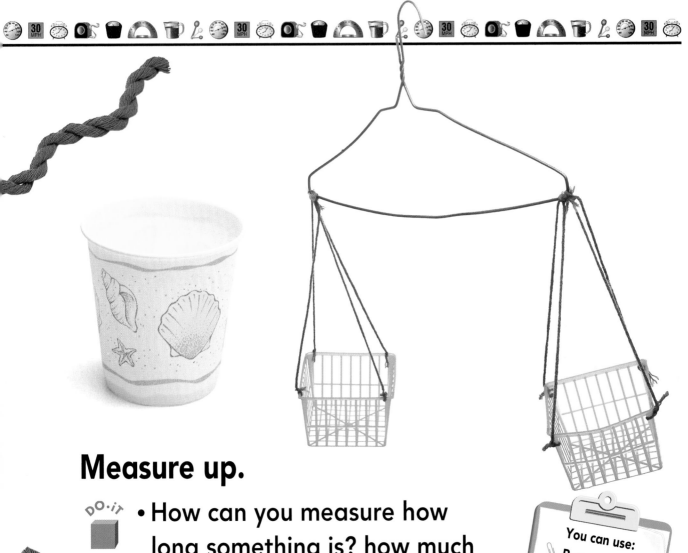

Measure up.

DO·IT
- How can you measure how long something is? how much something will hold? Invent a measuring tool to help you.
- Measure different classroom objects with your tool.

SHARE·IT
- Make a report to the class. Describe what you measured.

BUILD·ON·IT
- Invent some other tools. Use them to measure the things you described in your report.

You can use:
Paper-clip chain
Snap cubes
Yarn or string
Paper cup

THINK

How many different ways can you measure a paper towel?

How Will You Store Your Tools?

It is important to store your tools. Tool kits and toolboxes come in different shapes and sizes. What will yours be like?

18

Gear up.

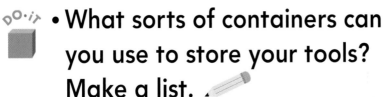 • What sorts of containers can you use to store your tools? Make a list.

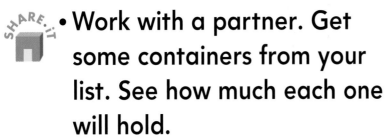 • Work with a partner. Get some containers from your list. See how much each one will hold.

• Which would you rather have — a toolbox, a tool belt, or a backpack? Make whichever one you choose.

You can use:
- Different containers
- Blocks
- Snap cubes
- Counters

THINK

Which holds more, a bag that holds five apples or one that holds twenty grapes?

Scout Mission #1:

Can You Find Objects of Equal Length?

Are you ready for scout missions? When you have completed these missions, you will be a full-fledged measurement scout.

You can use:
🖐 Your measurement tools

Find things of equal length.

DO·iT

• Find two things that are the same length. How long are they?

• How can numbers show that the things are equal in length?

HOW MUCH IS A MILLION?
by David M. Schwartz
pictures by Steven Kellogg

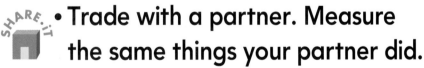

- Trade with a partner. Measure the same things your partner did.
- Did you and your partner make the same measurements? Write about how you measured.

- Try to find three things the same length. Write about them.

THINK

How can people compare their ages?

Scout Mission #2:

How Can You Measure a Basketball?

Some dinosaurs hatched from eggs as small as chicken eggs. Some dinosaurs hatched from eggs as big as basketballs. What else is round like a basketball?

Measure the ball.

DO·IT
- Work with a partner. Measure around the basketball.
- What else is that long?

You can use:
- Basketball
- Your measurement tools
- Paper
- Pencil

SHARE·IT
- Talk about what measurement tools you used.
- How else can you measure a basketball?

BUILD·ON·IT
- Estimate how big an orange is. Find out.
- How do the sizes of a basketball and an orange compare?

THINK

Why are basketballs round?

Scout Mission #3:

How Big Is Your Footprint?

One dinosaur footprint can be as big as a sandbox. About how many of these human footprints would it take to cover the dinosaur's footprint?

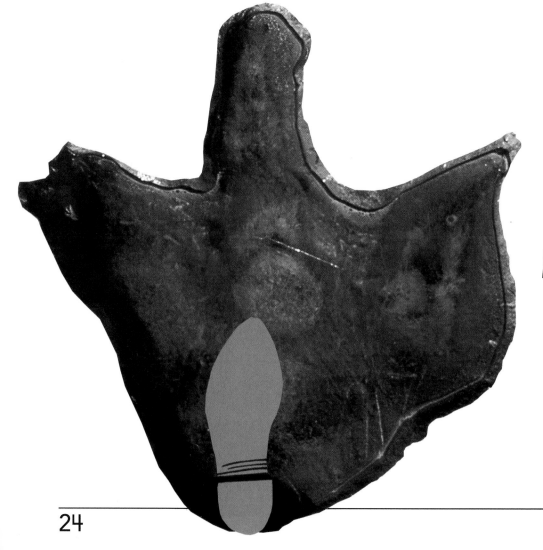

Put your foot down and measure.

DO·iT

- Work with a partner. Each of you trace a foot. Cut out your tracing.
- Estimate how many of your feet it would take to cover your desk. Then find out.

SHARE·iT

- Report to the class what you found out.
- Did your estimate help you? How?

BUILD·ON·iT

- If you put together every footprint in your class, how many desks could they cover?

You can use:
- Your feet
- Paper
- Pencil
- Scissors

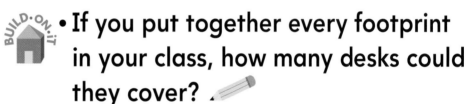

8 footprints cover my desk.

THINK
What else can you measure with your feet?

25

Scout Mission #4:
How Can You Compare Weights?

Take two things. How can you tell which one is heavier?

Weigh objects.

DO·iT
- Work with a partner. Pick two objects. Which one do you think weighs more? Find out.

You can use:
- Balance
- Objects in the classroom

SHARE·iT
- Show your results to the class.
- How are your results different from other kids' results? How are they the same?

BUILD·ON·iT
- How can you compare the weights of three things using a balance? Try it.

THINK

Are bigger things always heavier than smaller things? Explain.

Scout Mission #5:
How Big Will Your Canteen Be?

Scouts carry drinking water on hikes. Which of these containers will hold the most water? Which one would you rather carry on a hike?

Compare weight and capacity.

DO·iT
- Work with a partner. Find different containers that will hold water.
- Which holds the most? How do you know?

SHARE·iT
- Team up with another pair of scouts. Tell what you found.

BUILD·ON·iT
- Have a class meeting. Which containers would be best for each scout to carry on a hike? Why?
- Which containers would be best for a picnic? Why?

You can use:
- Different containers
- Water
- Smocks
- Paper towels
- Funnel

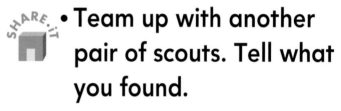

THINK

How many ways can you measure water?

Scout Mission #6:

How Long Does a Hike Take?

Scouts like to go on hikes. It takes time to hike from place to place. How long does it take to hike around your playground?

Names	Times
William	1 minute
David	17 minutes
Rebecah	9 minutes
Tom	27 minutes
Tina	22 minutes

You can use:
Stopwatch
Paper
Pencil
Crayons or markers

Time your hike.

- Go on a hike around your playground. Your teacher can time you.
- How long did your hike take?

- Work with a partner. Estimate about how long it would take to hike around the playground three times.
- Figure it out.
- Show how you found your answer.

- Estimate how long it takes you to get from home to school.
- Make a class chart with all the kids' times.

THINK
Does your chart tell you how far kids live from school? Why or why not?

How Did You Earn Your Measurement Badges?

You have been on many measurement missions. You earned many measurement scout badges. Make a display of what you did to earn your badges.